ECLIPSE OF THE SUN

University of Nevada Press | Reno, Nevada 89557 USA
www.unpress.nevada.edu
Copyright © 2023 by Paul Shuttleworth
All rights reserved
Manufactured in the United States of America

First Printing

Cover photograph © iStock/allanswart

Library Of Congress Cataloging-In-Publication Data
Names: Shuttleworth, Paul, 1944– author.
Title: Eclipse of the sun : boxing poems / Red Shuttleworth.
Description: Reno : University of Nevada Press, [2023] | Summary: "The poems within
Eclipse of the Sun offer homage to boxing at its grittiest levels and to fighters who
persevere, with hope, blood, and bone, against sense and loss. Few professional boxers
earn a living. Few world champion boxers arrive in their forties with any money left
from their sport. In Eclipse of the Sun, boxers arrive at poverty rather than riches, at
post-career menial jobs or worse, with no pension plan to fall back on. Perhaps the
luckiest are "journeymen," "opponents" who take on upcoming fighters—with little
hope of winning. These poems pay tribute to the improbable dreams of valiant men in a
rough sport."—Provided by publisher.
Identifiers: LCCN 2023002009 | ISBN 9781647791209 (paperback) | ISBN 9781647791216
(ebook)
Subjects: LCSH: Boxing—Poetry. | Boxers (Sports)—Poetry. | LCGFT: Poetry.
Classification: LCC PS3569.H865 E25 2023 | DDC372.270862—dc24/eng/20230125
LC record available at https://lccn.loc.gov/2023002009

The paper used in this book meets the requirements of American National Standard for
Information Sciences—Permanence of Paper for Printed Library Materials, ANSI/NISO
z39.48-1992 (R2002).

ECLIPSE OF THE SUN

boxing poems

RED SHUTTLEWORTH

UNIVERSITY OF NEVADA PRESS | *Reno & Las Vegas*

Contents

Ron Lyle vs. Muhammad Ali

Not a Contender, a Journeyman

Is you or is you ain't gonna give me a shot at the title?

—SONNY LISTON

If you're not willing to die, everything confuses you.
You got to be willing to die.

—TEDDY ATLAS

Have Fists Will Bang
Mackenzie, British Columbia

Nature's Course

Jab to the face, jab to the gut,
overhand to his head. . .
I win! First-round KO!

Shower. Meet Barry
at the Prince George Hotel.
Laugh. . .watch bar strippers
lazy-dance to an Elvis cassette,
"Suspicious Minds."

Four-round bouts.
Six-rounders.
Rare it works that way.

The Dog Knows Winter Is Coming

A creaking of fences.
The cows closer together.
Wood piles grow large.

Mothers walk children at a trot.

Below,
bones creak,
hug their bed.

The Boxer on Canvas

The grind of beaver teeth
back and forth over poplar.
I don't wake to blueberry pie,
huckleberries generously laced in,
vanilla ice cream on top.
No. A man is shouting down
a narrow coal mine shaft,
Seven. . .Eight. . .Nine. . .
And my knees won't listen,
my heart rushes blindly. . . .
I don't care about wood smoke
from slash fires I loved upon-a-time.
I cry to my deaf 'n dumb body
about gravity. Finally. . .I smile
at the people who want me to be
a vacant lot strewn with busted glass.

Prince George, BC, Canada:
Four-Round Bout

Earlier there was a drowned woman
pulled from a muskeg up in Mackenzie.
A squat 'n fat guy who talks New Jersey
says he's from *Ring Magazine*.

Pulp mill town. My tarot cards spell
anguish. I open with a six-punch combo,
follow him to a corner, no counterpunch.
Blurry vision since last April's snow.

I can still get a job selling fire extinguishers.
It's the second round. Three minutes are lost
from my life like steam out of a teapot.
The crowd whistles, chants for the other kid.

The local ref has a ruddy-pink masklike face.
The kid on the canvas has facial marbling.
The count is at seven. . .eight. I can still
get a job in Vancouver as a night watchman.

The Dog in the Cemetery

The gravestone in the rain.
The brambles over the body love the decay.

Visitors wish the name on the stone was theirs.

A dog circles a snowy sandbox
in a playground no child uses.
Arctic wind circles the dog.

I am a prizefighter. . .stunned. The ring
is knee-deep in snow. The odor of sweaty towels
drifts into the stadium from the forest.

The gravestone in the rain.
Happy with her ghosts, the widow
is sorry the children have their names.

Death cannot be lived up to.

The brambles shine in the rain,
a green luminous love.

Against the Sky on a Ridge

The echo of a crow
pumping wings in a blizzard.
A grizzly balances on a log.
Snowflakes on a cowboy hat
reflect yesterday's wintry sun.
A quiet Wolfhound parts snow,
is an ancient Celtic boat arriving.
Like a boxer from another century,
my blood is thick for joy.

Racing Our Seasons

In front of our shadow,
a cinnamon-red fox hesitates.
My Wolfhound springs,
loses the race. The fox
swerves off the snowy trail
into dense virgin forest.
The hound sniffs Arctic air.
I measure the tracks of the fox,
then the hound's, then mine
as if to know how close
true winter might be.

All-Night Prince George Waffle House. . .
Taking Rest

There's laughter in the Great Void.
That's concussion knowledge.

Screwball-energy hours after a fight,
you ask, *Was I brave?*

Your best side step, to an opponent's left,
is lost forever; right foot's gone jinxy.

The waitress is way-old, no round-card godiva,
I don't need to be a one-and-only.

Polished Walnut Coffin

Green-white glow
from a black bear skull
flashes off a photo
of a dead boxer.

Your muzzle
going forest gray,
you're learning
a road of wooden coffins.

It's an old bear's terror
when he touches the tag
a man has clipped
to a soft ear.

When you're dead,
the scars under the eyes
run away. . .into a soil
you know will blow away.

A Few Flakes of Snow Collapse

Locked. . .within my cranial vault,
I weave past familiar pines,
fall to a night in an empty cabin.

Drip of melting ice.
Conviction wears off like Portuguese wine.
But forget that. Tomorrow another wet
ghost-hand will shake
my shoulder to a tremble.

Friends, was it a random
drinking of amber booze that caught us
turning our hands from boxing gloves
abandoned in a blood-stained gym?

Noisy and distant starlight
demands miracle-of-nothing. . .
a constant dank morning
that denies night.

Evening at Crooked River, BC

The horror of leafless branches
glistening mud-brown in rain.
Moss-covered moose bones
on a wave of emerald weeds.

A dark cabin watches a lakelet.
Slime laps onto shore. . .glows.
The cabin's man listens for grizzly.

Rain comes in a torrent to the forest.
It's not an evening to be a stranger
trudging hooded to a settlement.
Mosquito dusk sinks into a water drop.

Hurricane, Eddie, Benny, Sonny, and Woody Woodpecker

Hurricane Jackson

Breakneck fighting pace, visibility
of personality as you took punishment
in bouts you were no longer good for.

Now. . .you drive a taxi toward
death-inevitable. You stroll
in front of a stranger's car. . .singing.

Today is for self-scrutiny of shadow boxing
in front of a gym mirror. . .a flurry of slaps
faking as jabs.

                              The mob owned you. . .

a manager called *Jimmy Spoons*
who took out eyeballs. You flailed,
could not bob or weave. . .after Patterson.

Street corner in Harlem. You ask strangers,
Wanna buy a botanical coat? You slip past
the real. . .dive into an ancient skeleton pit.

Eddie Machen

If you could've multiplied
that seventh round against Liston. . .

Sleepwalker.

Within your punched-out body,
you fell in love. . . . Sherry.
Done at boxing, you worked. . . .
Longshoreman. You swallowed
go-to-sleep pills with gulps
of Oly. Better the docks
than airport shoeshiner.

You kept to roadwork.
Out and back on the Golden
Gate Bridge. Memory only a jump
into pre-dawn water.

Asked about an interview,
you laughed at the *Examiner* reporter,
Used luggage got no talk to tell.

Sleepwalker.

Two pills and a bottle of Oly.
Sherry sleeps. You slip in beside
her, Italian perfume in her hair.
Sleepwalker. You shove
a love seat aside, climb out
a window. . . . Two-story dive. . .
no canvas to bounce up from. . .
walk on nothing. . .
nothing at all.

New York '58. . .Benny Kid Paret
Takes Up Residence at an Efficiency Hotel

Sparring at Stillman's,
you wake with soot on your blanket. . .
a case of chronic suffer-head.

Back home Castro is beating Batista.
Here on 42nd Street a girl walks by,
skirt cut below her knees, tan blazer,
blue scarf, sunglasses. Gape and shudder.

When not training or sleeping,
you ride department store escalators.
I am going up, I am going up, I am going
to the top. . .fights at St. Nicholas Arena.

A nice girl strips at a Village club. . .
coral-colored dance moves. Dangling
pay phone. . .no money to call Havana.

The Farm

I am a country boy. It is my aim to own
a farm someday. . .near a river.

—Benny Kid Paret

The baby Jesus rode
sidesaddle
right past your dreams.
And there is no river.
How simple.
It is the rhythm of a speed bag
handled with authority.
When we lose,
we discover stairs
downward to a parking lot.
As the lights are turned off,
iron stanchions glow luminous
around the necks of cattle.
Then the darkness of surgical drills,
the quiet of a broken toy.

Construction Sites. . .Blocked
Sidewalks. . .Pedestrian Detours

Look upon me. Look upon me. There will be
no copies. Every day: perfect intensity.
In the hotel before a walk to the gym,
television voices. Disembodied.

Pre-fight physical: strong pulse, a doctor
from one of the oasis neighborhoods.
Fight. Fight or starve. No long breaks.
Safety equals moral decline, teaches Fidel.

You have no sense, Benny, of ethereal gravity.
Wandering East 72nd you find an Easter basket
filled with pearly white. . .small pigeon bones.
A fifty-dollar girl smiles, *Let's put bow to string.*

Sometimes You Win. . .Big

Haunted arena.
Theatrical threads of meaning.
I longed to meet you, she says.

. . . just around the next blood-corner. . . .

You are in that little shop in the Village. . .
sampling chocolates on a summer morning.
You are showing off a bloody, broken nose.

. . . pale mannequin from last month's *Vogue.* . . .

It's never what people think, she tells you.
You tell her she has a. . .volatile body.
You kiss in a jewelry store mirror.

. . . voice like a screaming gull. . . .

Sometimes a fighter dies. Then
comes a funeral. *We're gonna work good
together,* says a new trainer. *Lots of dime candy.*

You're Dead When They Cut the Gloves Off

Around the time Bobby Gleason nailed
a portrait of Ike on his gym wall,
Saturday night meant TV boxing.
Even when he lost and died,
I worshipped the puncher
with iron will.
Benny Kid Paret, this poem
about velvet shark-fin eyes
snapping into the deep skull
of our roadwork dreams
is for you, gladiator.
It's also for me
as I look for the fine deed
battered onward without whiskey
or salvation. I'm trying to
hear the last right hook.

Watching the Bout on TV, Benny Kid Paret's Two-Year-Old Son Screamed: Papa...Papa...Papa...

Dry leaves skitter against the door.
That's what I hear. But if I step
into the float-away night to look,
white bone chips from a skull
will snow-drift about my boots.

It is the absence of echo...
the buzz of a surgeon drilling
for blood clots as if they were
tiny fists swinging against jelly.

You the Better Man?

Learn to exhale with every punch.

It is Christmas. Dreamlike mirrors in store windows.
Forgotten fighters sleep in subway stations,
pissy doorways, gutters of dim streets.

Exhale with every punch.

Benny takes the train to Long Island.
Boarded-up houses in Levittown.
He mugs a grocer's son for a pigskin wallet. . .
two dollars and a photo of his bedpan girlfriend.

With every punch. . . .

When the roof of life is on fire,
when your face is concussive purple,
when the girl stutters, says she is Sienna. . . .

Exhale. Exhale. Like sexual ecstasy.

Precise Jabs, a Hook to His Ribs

Aspirin. Bags of ice. Sleeping with a towel-wrapped
Bible as a pillow. It's a dirty dishes apartment.

You get your first body-shot knockout. The guy went
down hard, got back to his knees at the count of seven. . .
then keeled over as if to say, *Give me a minute, okay?*

Dinner: day-old French bread moist with olive oil.

The grocer's daughter bites her nails, asks,
What is it I look like, Broadway or Hollywood?
You're paid a hundred dollars for the body KO.

East 70s: fires in trash cans, tiny apartments
for out-of-work actors. You're a club fighter. . .

on a river of death. At the gym, an old fighter slurs,
What's the use? That won't be you in a nowhere.
Rockefeller Center. . .Christmas lights at midnight.

Three Days Beyond Leotis Martin
vs. Sonny Banks

For Lucien Banks, Philadelphia no longer exists.
The hardwood timberland on Birmingham Ridge
has fallen into darkness and there's no road
home to that gone-shack between Tupelo and Saltillo.

Paring fingernails on the train back to New York,
the ringside touts fold newspaper sheets
against cigar ash. A trinity of nuns, two fat and
one skinny, cough. . .rub unreliable eyes.

Sickening skull bone crack. . .three days with a clot.
This is not sleep. Lunge and punch and. . .drop.
The ref counts to ten like a dull knock-knock joke.
Sonny once bragged, *I only get small ailments.*

In Philly, a midnight payphone rings. . .no answer.

Woody Woodpecker

Got his name from a semi-weak jab.
Statue of Liberty from a ferry
on Monday mornings to see lady tourists.
So much gets lost. . .is lost.

Melancholy train rides out to Long Island,
January beaches, moody with feigned stupidity
like a young punch-drunk.

Finally, a girl, garment district receptionist,
invites him home, situates Woody in a chair. . .
undresses, gets dressed, undresses. . .over and over.

Cheap bourbon instead of mouthwash
in the mouthpiece jar. Dreams of home:
wildfire smoke. . .turkey vulture skies:
Woody never hedges a goddamn bet.

Hospital Bed in a Living Room

On the TV girls in ratty gray rabbit fur jackets
are parading a busy street out west in LA.
Girls, he says to no one. *Always ask for a phone number.*

Hazy day outside. Hicksville. A private house
half-cramped as a miniature rest home.
Sometimes his eyes click and get smeary.

He remembers a Manhattan museum. . .
Roman helmets in glass cases.
Like blood-filled spit buckets.

Later, before this TV day on Burns Ave.,
living in insomniac rooms by the month,
he had an even record after a dozen bouts.

Half dozen to the good, half dozen all wrong.
He remembers a smeared-makeup girl,
her tongue inside his mouth, her gift for tears.

On the TV, boys in varsity jackets dance in a line.
The music is ossified. The dancers grimace.
See, he says, *always get the girl's number.*

Ron Lyle vs. Muhammad Ali

Carrying the Baggage

—for Kate

A night wind off the Mojave
tastes of your tangerine kisses.
Miles shift between hawks.
The glide of a summer hand
over apricot skin is everything
until no breath is left.
My hands must never become
arithmetic in textbooks.
A portrait of a nude
is on my motel room wall,
done with rose petals stuck together
with moonlit pine sap.
If I shout, *Regret,*
a hawk will carry the word
to you. . .wherever you love.
I'm learning to help
when I can.

South. . .A Mile Short of True Vegas

Hitcher girl says, *I enjoy money.*
She's in a tea-stain wedding dress.
I enjoy, she smiles, *showin' all my flavors.*

You're headed for the Trop. . .even though
the Lyle camp chuckled, said they don't
need you as a sparring partner for Ron.

You can use a fight-day breakfast:
sausage 'n banana, jug of fruit-juicy punch.
Later: sleep. . .bloody-pissed hotel linen.

Mock-Hollywood femmes fatales, common
boxing brain injuries, old-at-25 middleweights
as placard wavers on lonesome street corners.

Roadwork, Six Miles with Ron Lyle in Las Vegas, at the Dunes Golf Course, a Few Days Prior to Lyle's World Championship Bout with Muhammad Ali

No fear in the pre-dawn.
No flinching, but I wonder if rattlesnakes
are playing the sand traps. Lyle, hooded gray,
is a tight whirlpool, wordless, and we're merely
strides from the first chip-songs of morning

* * *

Sparring partners shuffle-churn the silence.
Shadows thin moment by green grassy moment.
We burst up soft hills, Lyle now thudding-fast.
My thoughts whip northeast to wild horse country.
Suddenly the memory of a grizzly outside
of Mackenzie, BC, a big fellow
who insisted on one more day of hibernation.

* * *

Bear? Lyle is a dancing bear. . .fight touts
flabby and lungs sprung from cigs. . .a dancing bear
in tune with coming-upon-us dry lightning.
Lyle is ready to try his gift in any weather.
He is now running loose, at ease with his days.
My side aches, but I sprint, fast as Lyle,
to witness how a man prepares
for a Mojave-spring downpour.

The Workhouse

(The Workhouse was the nickname given to the Folies Bergere Room at the Tropicana Hotel in Las Vegas by visiting boxers. In the weeks before their fight, Ron Lyle and Muhammad Ali, and their sparring partners, used the room for sparring and floorwork.)

The ring ropes are purple velvet, the same shade
of velvet worn by sleek Black girls who're more,
much more, than blonde. Ali begins his work. . .
dancing. . .dancing. . .dancing. . .through ghost-
generations of showgirls. Ali shuffle-skips
through refracted light of mystic sequins.

* * *

The workhouse is left alone this morning.
It is so quiet that I walk past ten years
of my world. An hour passes:
middle-aged men appear in the yellowish
audience seating area. Children show up.
The crowd has come to see Ali make faces. . .
recite his verse.

                    I leave for a sandwich. . .

twenty bucks' worth of one-arm bandit pulls.
I return with Ron Lyle, sparring partners
Leroy Jones and Johnny Boudreaux.
Lyle never acknowledges the curious crowd,
I'm catching my life on the ropes.

Lyle vs. Ali, Tenth Round

Ahead on points, having staggered Ali
with a right cross in the ninth, Lyle is stunned
by a flurry of soft punches, then 21 unanswered
stronger head-shots. No cut men needed.
Both faces are in good shape. Lyle's trainer,
Chickie Ferrara (*Joggers in shorts deserve
arthritis!*), shouts at the referee,
Why'd you stop the fight? The crowd leaves
for the one-armed bandits. Empty arena.

Melancholia in Lyle's after-fight room.
Every dream has a breaking point.
Blind anxieties toward tomorrow.
Lyle nods to handler Mike Hayes. . .
sportswriters are let into the room.
Soft questions in washed-out blue tones.
The writers want an easy cartoon narrative
to finger-churn on a typewriter.

For Lyle. . .scarring of his heart,
unwanted, yet offered, pity and sorrow
from two old Canon City fellow inmates.
For Lyle. . .a lights-dim flight back to Denver,
hardly even a contender after this TKO.

Dreams linger beneath summer aspen.
Lyle believes there might be other shots
at the heavyweight title. He does not
own the gift of weeping. Lyle will be left
hanging off the ropes of impossibility
as Ali shuffles into tremors. . .slurred prayer.

A Taped Jump Rope Dangles
in the Night Gym

Boxing gloves ear-out from a wall with crimson pegs.
The name *Sugar Moon* is fading off a glossy pine door
that's cracked from a lost man's right cross.
It's a ringside dimming of fast shadows gone blind.

Not a Contender, a Journeyman

Night Train

Done with cleaning flooded basements, you roll
in a window seat, no sleeper berth. Wrenched neck,
maybe a broke power-side hand, scratched retina:
you're a boxer, freest man since they gutted Jesus Christ.

Rolling through towns and farmland, small fires
in trash cans, vacant brick factories, mutual distrust. . .
the train conductor and you. Back in Cheyenne,

after a four-round split decision win against a boy
whose pregnant wife sat ringside, you bought
a lime-green cowboy shirt with a matching Stetson.

It is a night of twin moons, one on each side
of the Missouri River. Memory of a Jefferson, Iowa,
casino fight. . .dung flies over a chef salad, water-
stained Coca-Cola glass filled with cig butts.

Spokane

Don't speak my opponent's
Christian name. Don't tell me
'bout his three kids, the wife
who can't graduate nursing school.
Don't say his three kids are all
gonna need braces, and one kid
has half a case of leukemia.

If you die before you die...

Tell me more about his bad knees,
lack of lateral mobility, his weight gain
since his last fight two long years ago...
all the donuts 'n guzzlin' Rainier
by the rack weekdays 'n Sundays.

If you die before...

Don't tell me about the guy's
long, long shifts cooking fries
with pancakes at a roadhouse.
Better to know he starts with
head-hunting hooks...that
he can be jabbed to distraction,
killed with an overhand right.

If you die...

Your last memory could be
tattered, taped Spokane ring ropes.
Your next memory could be
an intensive care nurse
named for an Irish river.
If you die, there might be hope.

Faith, Whirligig, Damnation

The noisy moon of childhood never sets.
I phoned to sacrifice my blushing horizon.
She was angled on her bed, Raitt was *Come
here go away*: there was little to ask for.

Buck deer are losing antlers. A month
of flipped nickels. . .greenish meteors.
I'm fumbling with *lessness*. . .
hawking songs of punch drunk.

Extra Blanket

Other day in Fayetteville, a pair of lean college girls
were parading in tight white jeans. . .teeny halters.
Not that much younger than me, but that much younger.
Know what I mean?

                      What's fame but a personalized
headstone, an extra blanket against January nights. . . .
Continuity of life fades into each sunfall's darkness.

But. . .when I step into a boxing ring. . .glare another
prizefighter in the eye, we're like ancient
Homeric gods, warriors from a rougher, braver time.
That's one hellaciously wonderful *Insatiable* that I own.

Sun is stuttering-up quick on the plains east of Denver. . .
tangerine hue and then jaundice yellow through thin clouds.
Maybe a punched-down buffoon some nights,
but there's never a bout on Sundays, *The Lord's Day,*

a trainer once said to me, a guy who locked his gym
that one day a week. He used to say, *Faith just can't
be a façade.* Pro boxing beats a chicken-kill plant.

Union City, Tennessee, Six Rounds

Cut flowers in a crystal vase. The motel office. . .
windows sealed by age, paint, rain-hardened warp.

Simple combo gets you by. . .over and over:
left-right, left-right, left hook to the ribs,
a side step and a right to the side of his head.

Upturned collars at the cemetery. Some old man
buried: like many of my father's blood. . .Manley,
Cloys, Baty, Lint Stewart who fathered dozens.

On a south wind, songs from the further shore.
Weightless strangers of my blood stand beside me,
ghost-linger beneath winter trees, no thrust or rapture.

In my corner, a pock-marked spit bucket man.
No man. . .no true man. . .speaks of his fear.
No. He speaks hard 'n cruel to his fear.

Roadwork in the rain or a day of not eating. Got to
make weight in a dead window-flies town.

Holy Mass for Broken Hands

Stale donuts. . .cold no-sugar black tea.
That motel is jammed between tattoo parlors.

Bikini Babe. . .the last two-week wife. . .
She liked to lick my face. . .marmalade spread on it.

A fighter is best devoted to loneliness.
Chickie Ferrara told me, *Love that roadwork alone.*

The priest at St. Pat's ate silvery fish tails. . .
slept with a threadbare second-hand teddy bear.

Once saw a reliquarium in a Polish church.
Saint's wrist bone. Gristle-stained a taffy brown.

Undercard fighter reaches Vegas totally alone.
When Jesus finally chose. . .He shortened the day.

Flash a Smile and Keep Walking

How often we meet a guy who wants
slices of bread from the middle of loaves.

Once in Reno I slept in a cardboard
fridge box. . .near the Siena by the Truckee.

A deep rugged mountain gorge: retracing events
from fried squirrel bits. . .childhood. . .to the ring.

We are in the Age of Diagrams. I'm free of that.
A rising, ornery full moon. Dark ocher boulders.

I'm half an hour from flying over Sonny Liston.
Vegas casino TV bouts: Darwinism in the desert.

Characters of the Hilton Sports Book: a novelist
dry for decades, carny barkers, age-useless gangsters. . . .

On the outside of thought, on thought's freckled skin,
forward-fighting, snap-jabs, body hooks are wisdom.

Eclipse of the Sun

A woman chain-smokes. Bus station. . .Nashville.
Gray ash of the moon. Skyscrapers. Haven't
noticed clouds in weeks. . . . Last fight was
more pushing and shoving than punching.

I'm thirty-three. . .or thirty-seven
if honesty is a dollar. Back in New York,
another old fighter is on the midnight
subway in a sauna suit. . .making weight.

Between coasts, at behind-closed-door bouts,
I take a flat five hundred. . .take it easy
on locals. . .losses not going on my record.
The gestures of murder minus any results.

Riding buses, I stick to berries, fast burgers
(no buns), cheapest bottled water. *I don't know
nothin' outside a boxing.* For small-town paper
interviews, you smile out of a snarl.

Visits with Joanna

She brings me home, royal blue
rolled-arm sofa. . .velvet.
Apartment 3R, on East 39th,
off Lexington. Art Deco bed. . .
lacquered walnut, brass, leather.
Upstairs. . .into clouds.

Garden lunch at MOMA.
She pays with *Vogue* money. . .
her pic on the cover.
Joanna slow-sips Pernod
at Stefan's in the Village.
I have tap water on ice,
squeeze of lemon.

I win a four-round
undercard at the Arena.
In the cab, scent of jasmine.
In her kitchen, homemade
brownies and iced water.

Joanna is a head taller. . .
carries less weight,
uses a sleep mask. . .
likes darkness.

Two weeks. Eventide.
A taxi to the Gramercy
Park Hotel. . .she shows me
my new room. . .paid for.
Joanna says, *Ever go to Rome,*
drop by if you're not punch-drunk.

Peppermint Go-Go Ancient Diary

Sun-splashed Central Park. *Vogue* models take
Plaza Hotel lunch. *All the Way with LBJ.*

Old fighter at Stillman's. Heavy sedation shuffle.

Summer soot all across the room. . .on clothes.
Sweat with black specks. Simple window fan breaks.

Pair of used ten-ounce gloves for bag work.

Pay five. Girl struts room in beaded moccasins. . .
naked. That's all for five. . .no kiss.

Leave the gym. Walk half a night. Dazzling
charity ball gowns at the Waldorf. . .joker-card.

Small park squirrels. . .in olive oil. . .borrowed fry pan.

Got a match? asks a yellow-teeth corner girl.

Wealthy means tree-lined cobblestone streets.

Free dinner at Elaine's. Thank you, Joanna.

Strained right thumb. Left shoulder ache
from bag work. . .hook-finish combos.

Bar. Ice water 'n lemon. Françoise Hardy
on Scopitone juke. . ."All the Boys and Girls."

More often than not. . . .

Same silence. . .in a long shower.

Overgrown Memory

Avoid weeds of malicious intent. No fights
outside the ring: so often stoned on memory.
Canary sky. Nude girls with silver bracelets.

Sunbathers in a Vegas casino parking lot. . .roped-off.
Security faces outward. Burnt orange cliffs. Texas
Longhorn skulls. . .after-dinner mints. Dry kisses.

In my somewhere-else-time, amber lanterns,
pink glass beads. Live chickens in a butcher store
window. . .and a blind piglet. I pine for adrenaline.

A final and last bout: bug-eyed third-row women,
fatty tits and bulge-bellies. . .low-cut tops, summer dresses.
At least there's no whiplash of the brain stem.

Night Watchman. . .One-Eyed Attack Dog Mutt

After chasing dollars as a palooka, seven times KO'd
in a week of dives at five hundred each—
gotta love Iowa—I'm patrolling a Salina factory,
minimum wage. . .a single-wide trailer for insomnia.

Last security guard got caught jacking off to a ballet
poster. Couldn't take snowy nights of small, cheap
padlocks to test. I make endless circuits
where no one has a clue what's manufactured.

Torn jeans, uniform shirt, and blue cop jacket,
Salvation Army running shoes. . .and it's good enough
to bob-'n-weave forward, toss jabs at half-shadows
of myself, to spin, sidestep, come in with an uppercut.

I get old enough and there's nothing left: regional
title belt sold to a KC hock shop, two or three gone-wives
no more useful than a snub-nosed revolver, not one bullet.
Clean bed, good trailer roof, no one knows my name.

Last Day of Summer

Neck muscles tighten. I rummage a closet
for sweatpants and a sweatshirt.

                              Bartender
could be next. Or splintered skull bone. Or

the old rotary phone rings for the ninth round. . .
fog-veil. . .stench of a dead, pissed-in phone booth.

Grandfather bought Stanley Ketchel's teeth,
but it was a scam. Angelo Dundee said, *You fight*

like a guy in handcuffs. No, you never did get
that sparring partner job. You trudge six dawn miles.

Roadwork in hiking boots. Asked to donate
posthumous brain tissue, *This is the way it'll be.*

September, old mattress on the floor. Maybe-wife
blurts, *No way. I don't even know you no more.*

Sparring in a Cold Showers Gym

Learning the invasive life
of feather grass,
the prizefighter
listens to a Waylon song
inside a bottle of Lone Star.
Winter is here with
windblown brittle leaves.
The prizefighter gives up
dyeing his beard dark.
Up the street a sale
on glass-top caskets.
He wakes before dawn
halfway through a scream.

January Roadwork: Watery, Red Eyes

Squirrel pie. . .sweet 'n sour sauce.
Lumpy boxer face, grief for the dead, dust of inner rooms. . . .

I'm a sculpture crafted of bison rib cages. . .
shot through with passing headlights.

Casino town of cracked windshields. A sensation of body fade
to bone particle. . .gristle. I shadowbox ghosts.

The Further Days

April elation, bourbon, and luck:
a stop in Missoula, Eddie's Club. . .
Lee Nye portraits of dead patrons.

Later. . .a knife wins over a pool stick
in Browning. Every KO has a loophole.
Wilting graveyard flowers in a ditch.

Loose-tethered on day-to-day necessities,
a second-round hook to a kid's right kidney. . .
he drops like a stack of hoarded magazines.

Way past 37, I need an EKG. . .an MRI
of my brain. Forgeries make legitimacy.
Four-round bouts. . .crinkled paper money.

In a decade. . .a collage of brutal bouts. . .
flashes of skull-light, day duties of lucidity
lost like mailbox keys in a jam jar cupboard.

The incomparable power of someone else's
blood on canvas. Glimmer-moon. . .faint clouds.
I finally call. She says, *Here we fuckin' go again.*

Afterlife Road

Autumn. Ragged wheat. . .grazing deer.
A hollow man might fill himself with gravel.

I don't sleep as I did before dying.
Sunday bells and weeds to resolve.

What chance does any sunset really have?

Low Rounds. . .High-Intensity Workout

What you saw as a child, the fighter dying on TV,
had a gurgle to it. Such is memory. . .black & white.

Slips of paper passed from girl to girl, sometimes
grabbed by a boy: experience as trellised roses.

I'm sitting with buttered crackers, checking
local weather predictions, daydream of pouting

French lips. . .Léa Hélène Seydoux. That's why public
buildings have fire extinguishers in lilac-gloom corners.

I'm trying to shorten punches, throw leapfrog
rights over left jabs. . . . I'm nowhere near myself.

Dementia Pugilistica

Are you my friend?
I got cadaver-blue knuckles and a silk handkerchief
if I need to blow my nose. How many stitches you ever take?

It's early June. . .wind in sagebrush.
Could we be old friends? New York? Yes, sir.
Garbage pickup day. . .lines of dented trash cans.
And we had lunch at the Plaza Hotel, Tuesdays. . .

me 'n Jerry Coleman. He was a Yankee once. . .
dated a girl name of Anna, like to senior prom.
It ain't toy-store rubber snakes that night-visit.
In the middle of dying, I always remember.

Could we be old friends?
These days I sell green apples off a truck.
I preloaded a few punches. . .was caught on my head.

After I Die...

I'm gonna drive up 'n down the fuckin'
Ghost Road with Sonny and Benny Kid. . .
listenin' to James Brown do "Night Train."

We're gonna drink J&B.
We're gonna be in Sonny's '63
cream-color Fleetwood Caddy.
We're gonna be with perfumed
fine women, you know, sweet
as Hostess turnover cherry pies. . . .

After I die, I'm comin' back before Jesus,
to grin 'n growl, redeem Benny Kid. . .
comin' back a huge 'n hungry gray wolf.

Acknowledgments

Caledonia Writing Series: "Watching the Bout on TV, Benny Kid Paret's Two-Year-Old Son Screamed: Papa. . .Papa. . .Papa. . ."

Confrontation: "Carrying the Baggage"

Dacotah Territory: "A Few Flakes of Snow Collapse"

Jeopardy: "You're Dead When They Cut the Gloves Off"

The Other Side of the Shouting: "Lyle vs. Ali, Tenth Round" was published as "Ron Lyle's 10th Round Against Mohamad Ali"

Poetry Now: "The Dog Knows Winter Is Coming," "The Boxer on Canvas," and "Evening at Crooked River, BC"

Rapport: "The Dog in the Cemetery"

Repository: "Against the Sky on a Ridge" and "Racing Our Seasons"

Sam Houston Literary Review: "The Farm"

San Pedro River Review (republished): "The Farm"

Texas Portfolio: "Sparring in a Cold Showers Gym" was published as "Boxing in a Gym Where the Showers Are Cold"

"Carrying the Baggage" was part of the sequence "Journey," in *Western Settings*, published by University of Nevada Press in 2000.

A chapbook, *Poems to the Memory of Benny Kid Paret*, was published by Felix and Selma Stefanile's Sparrow Press in 1978. The present collection came from a desire to revisit that work, which included "The Dog Knows Winter Is Coming," "The Boxer on Canvas," "The Dog in the Cemetery," "You're Dead When They Cut the Gloves Off," "Watching the Bout on

TV, Benny Kid Paret's Two-Year-Old Son Screamed: Papa. . . Papa. . . Papa. . . ," "Against the Sky on a Ridge," "Racing Our Seasons," "A Few Flakes of Snow Collapse," "Carrying the Baggage," "Roadwork, Six Miles with Ron Lyle in Las Vegas, at the Dunes Golf Course, a Few Days Prior to Lyle's World Championship Bout with Muhammad Ali," "Lyle vs. Ali, Tenth Round" (previously titled "Ron Lyle's 10th Round Against Mohamad Ali"), "A Taped Jump Rope Dangles in the Night Gym," "Evening at Crooked River, BC," "Polished Walnut Coffin" (previously titled "Wooden Coffin"), and "Sparring in a Cold Showers Gym" (previously titled "Boxing in a Gym Where the Showers Are Cold").

Much is owed to the late Margaret Dalrymple, who helped me craft this book from the first version. Margaret was part of the splendid, heady days, a couple of decades ago, at University of Nevada Press. A wise voice for books-in-progress, a dear optimist, a patient and wise counselor, Margaret was a true-heart, selfless editor.

As with a preceding book, *Hardly Alone,* daughter Ciara Shuttleworth has been essential in numerous ways and matters. Ciara has been essential as my personal editor when health concerns required that I step away for periods of time.

About the Author

RED SHUTTLEWORTH holds degrees from City College of San Francisco, San Francisco State University, and the University of Nevada, Las Vegas. He has been writing poetry for more than fifty years and has also written short fictions and plays for more than three decades. Shuttleworth taught college-level English, which is when he took up boxing. He had three amateur bouts, one of which he won by decision. At the age of seventy-five, Shuttleworth began training again to box and now has a 2-0 record, with one win by a first-round knockout and the other by decision. Both matches were against boxers in their twenties.